YOUR KNOWLEDGE HAS VALUE

Sabrina Wirz

The Future of Outer Space Security

GRIN Verlag

Bibliografische Information der Deutschen Nationalbibliothek:

Die Deutsche Bibliothek verzeichnet diese Publikation in der Deutschen National-
bibliografie; detaillierte bibliografische Daten sind im Internet über http://dnb.d-
nb.de/ abrufbar.

Imprint:

Copyright © 2011 GRIN Verlag GmbH
Druck und Bindung: Books on Demand GmbH, Norderstedt Germany
ISBN: 978-3-656-34634-0

This book at GRIN:

http://www.grin.com/en/e-book/206494/the-future-of-outer-space-security

GRIN - Your knowledge has value

Der GRIN Verlag publiziert seit 1998 wissenschaftliche Arbeiten von Studenten, Hochschullehrern und anderen Akademikern als eBook und gedrucktes Buch. Die Verlagswebsite www.grin.com ist die ideale Plattform zur Veröffentlichung von Hausarbeiten, Abschlussarbeiten, wissenschaftlichen Aufsätzen, Dissertationen und Fachbüchern.

Visit us on the internet:

http://www.grin.com/

http://www.facebook.com/grincom

http://www.twitter.com/grin_com

Sabrina Wirz
Université de Toulouse M2 RIPS

THE FUTURE OF OUTER SPACE SECURITY

As one gazes up at the stars on a clear night, tracing constellations or wishing on a shooting star, it is unlikely that most of us would stop to reflect on the role this once distant and mysterious realm plays in our contemporary world today. Nor would we pause to reflect on the possible threats that might endanger it and our comfortable way of life that we have grown so accustomed to. Often portrayed as the doorway to mythic worlds, outer space held until very recently, the title of the last frontier. However during this past century, mankind has set out to explore the shores of a new world, just as Christopher Columbus did five centuries ago. And just as these former pioneers found with the Americas a world of opportunity and exploration, so have our modern day scientists and astronauts, discovered the same with outer space. It is with this exploration of our last frontier that we have been able to make scientific advances and discoveries that have so profoundly shaped the world we know. Early on in this human adventure, world leaders realized the potential for greed and selfishness to destroy the delicately established common community which recognized no nation's colors. It was with this in mind, at the beginning of the US and USSR space race that US President Eisenhower stated: "I propose that we agree that outer space should be used only for peaceful purposes. We face a decisive moment in history in relation to this matter.... Should not outer space be dedicated to the peaceful uses of mankind and denied to the purposes of war?"[1] Fifty years after this statement, we are faced with the ever-increasing militarization of space and the possibility of space weaponization. Despite general worldwide consent that the prevention of space weapons is imperative in ensuring relative security in outer space, progress towards this objective has been disheartening. The inherent structure of the international system as well as recent non-cooperative actions and attitudes displayed by the world's powers, leave little hope for Eisenhower's proposition, made those fifty years ago. The comprehensive security of outer space is threatened, and with that so are the substantial benefits that mankind has reaped from its use.

I will in this paper argue that space weaponization is inevitable and consequentially then so is an outer space arms race. In order to fully understand the implications of this statement as well as the logic behind this argument, it is important to have a general understanding of the role of space in our world today, as well as to have a comprehensive concept of space security and the general threats facing it. Therefore, before providing the arguments to support my hypothesis, I will provide the reader with a comprehensive summary of the current space situation and relevant concepts tied to it. I then will focus on the specific threat of space weaponization and an outer space arms race. A discussion concerning a comprehensive definition of what constitutes a space weapon will be provided as will a prediction of the devastating consequences of such weapon deployment. This will be followed by an overview

---

[1] S. Estabrooks « Opposing weapons in space », *The Ploughshares Monitor, 23.3, Sept. 2002.*

of preventative measures that have been taken against the deployment of space weapons, as well as the effectiveness of these measures. After this basic summary of the current outer space situation has been established, I will analyze the likelihood of space weapons deployment in the future, based on recent international trends as well as the national space policies of influential states. I will subsequently support my conclusion that space weaponization and a space arms race are inevitable by providing theoretical arguments that prove this point.

In order to fully understand the devastating effects space weaponization would have on our world, it is important to be conscientious of the vast and diverse roles outer space use plays in today's contemporary society.

USES OF OUTER SPACE

Commonly considered 'the last frontier', outer space is a vast mass of potential for discovery that mankind, although having advanced a lot, still knows very little about. Since our first ventures into space nearly sixty years ago, technological advances have allowed the world community to make extraordinary achievements especially in the field of science. The benefits of space exploration, and our consequential use of space technology, are undeniable, as it has allowed us to gain a better understanding of our globe's environment. The use of satellites has allowed us to observe the Earth below sea level, at ground level, and in the air. It has allowed us to study changes in climate and provides us with valuable information concerning natural and man-made disasters such as forest fires, oil spills, and floods[2]. Furthermore, satellites play an essential role in the functioning of our infrastructure; whether it concerns public services, medical systems, financial services, police forces or the military.[3] In addition to providing essential and at times lifesaving information for various sectors, the use of satellites has revolutionized the way in which our world communicates. Wireless phones, the internet, and satellite television permit our world community to be connected to one another in ways never thought possible one century ago. The use of outer space activities has even spread to include commercial use. This proves to be a growing industry, with one third of all space launches being accounted for by the commercial sector.[4]

As the only common space that is shared by all countries, it is evident that outer space is a complex field with many uses and actors involved. The peaceful uses of outer space, which have been mainly focused on scientific advancement and discovery, are very valuable to all nations and citizens on Earth, whether involved in space activities or not. Sixty years after this space adventure began; there are more than 125 countries involved in various space activities and close to 780 spacecraft currently deployed in the near-Earth space environment.[5]

Yet within this maze of scientific discovery and the use of satellite technology for development purposes, is the often overlooked exploitation of technological advancements for

---

[2] A. Arbatov, Outer Space : Weapons, Diplomacy and Security (Washington, D.C., 2010) 4.
[3] Cesar Jaramillo, "Space Security Fact Sheet" *Space Security Index*, 2010, Web.
[4] S. Estabrooks « Opposing weapons in space »
[5] Arbatov xxi.

2

military purposes. Around forty percent of the spacecraft currently in orbit are active military satellites. A large proportion of these satellites are the possession of the USA, yet NATO allies, as well as Russia, have also deployed satellites serving military purposes. [6] Such satellites main role is to provide military forces with information that will aid them in their land, sea and air missions.[7] The use of satellites for defensive purposes by the military has been accepted over the past fifty years as comprising part of the 'peaceful uses of outer space'. This claim has been justified by the fact that the satellites used for military operations, possess no destructive capabilities on their own.[8]

Our world's ever-increasing and evident dependence on satellites span almost all sectors of modern day life. The undeniable advantages obtained through the unprecedented levels of knowledge concerning our environment that we have attained through the use of outer space related technology, should ignite within all an interest for the safekeeping of this vast common space. International cooperation on the scientific and commercial uses of space has been quite consistent and encouraging. However the vulnerability of satellites is reason for concern for countries such as the USA, who depend largely on satellite systems in order to carry out their military operations.[9] The military aspect of outer space thus provides incentive for outer space weapons systems that would protect such satellites but paradoxically, simultaneously create serious outer space security issues.

CONCEPT OF SPACE SECURITY

Given its essential role in a vast range of domains of modern life, as mentioned above, the security of satellite systems (essentially outer space security), has become an important part of national security concerns in nearly all developed nations.[10] Yet given the vast use of space, the uniqueness of its environment, and the rapidity with which technologies in this realm are advancing, creating a comprehensive definition of space security is a rather challenging task. Nevertheless, the Space Security Index (SSI), an organization initiated by the Government of Canada in response to a diplomatic deadlock concerning international cooperation on space security, has created a comprehensive definition of space security that seems to have been generally accepted worldwide.[11] The SSI states space security as "the secure and sustainable access to and use of space and freedom from space-based threats for *all actors* in space".[12] Using this definition, space security can be evaluated using nine different security indicators, which are; the s pace environment, laws and policies, civil space programs and global utilities, commercial space, space support for terrestrial military operations, space systems protection, space systems negation, space-based strike weapons, and space situational awareness.[13] These measures can further be categorized into three main areas which are; the operating

[6] Ibid. xxii
[7] Arbatov 12.
[8] S. Estabrooks « Opposing weapons in space »
[9] S. Estabrooks « Opposing weapons in space »
[10] Arbatov xxii.
[11] Jessica West « Reaching out : New approaches to security in space », *The Ploughshares Monitor, 30.1, Mar. 2009.*
[12] Cesar Jaramillo, "Space Security Fact Sheet"
[13] Ibid.

environment, actors and activities in space, and space technology. This widely accepted definition, mentioned above, provides a global concept of space security. It reflects a shift from the general traditional concept of security that focuses on the military, to a broader, more global concept of space security which takes into consideration the uses of military, civil and commercial actors.[14] This definition emphasizes the fact that outer space is a shared security as the environment of this vast shared space affects actors from all countries, and thus requires cooperation from mankind as a whole, if this precious last frontier is to remain one of discovery and not of threats.

THREATS TO SPACE SECURITY

Once the definition of space security has been defined, the most interesting and obvious next step is to assess the threats posed to space, given the established space security definition. The challenges to outer space security can be divided into two categories; environmental threats and deliberate threats (use of force in outer space).

   a) Environmental Threats

 The environmental threats are the inevitable result of the expansion of human outer space activities. The use of outer space by an ever-increasing number of countries has resulted in crowded orbits, a shortage of channels for frequency distribution, and an increase of space debris.[15] Environmental threats are thus not tied to any deliberate action, but to the changing space environment in which the increase of space traffic risks interference with or destruction of orbiting satellites. Although outer space may seem like a virtually unlimited space welcoming new spacecraft, there is in reality a limited number of orbits suitable for most satellite use. This means that the increase in outer space activities is taking place in a limited area, and thus increases the density of satellites in a given orbit, which in turn increases the probability of a collision.[16] This proved to be the case on February 10th, 2009, when an American and Russian spacecraft collided in low earth orbit.[17] This collision not only legitimized the fear of satellite collisions, it also brought to light the issue of the proliferation of space debris which is of particular concern to space security. There are currently over 19,000 objects 10cm in diameter or larger, orbiting the Earth, of which 90 percent are space debris. Such debris is extremely dangerous for orbiting satellites because travelling at speeds of 7.5 km per second, even the smallest pieces of debris can have a devastating impact on a spacecraft.[18] What complicates matters is that to date, there exists no way to remove this debris from its destructive path. Thus the effects of space debris risk having a compounding effect in which existing debris causes a collision which creates more debris, which in turn increases the chances of a future debris creating collision.[19] However international

[14] West "Reaching out : New approaches to security in space".
[15] Pan Jusheng, « Addressing the Outer Space Security Issue », UNIDIR, *Building the Architecture for Sustainable Space Security* (Conference Report) Mar. 2006.
[16] West « Back to the Future: The Outer Space Treaty turns 40 » *The Ploughshares Monitor, 28.3, Sept. 2007.*
[17] West "Reaching Out: New approaches to security in space".
[18] Cesar Jaramillo, "Space Security Fact Sheet"
[19] West « Fallout from China's anti-satellite test »*The Ploughshares Monitor, 28.1, Mar.2007.*

cooperation to address this environmental issue has been very encouraging. Pressure by the UN Committee on the Peaceful Uses of Outer Space and the Inter-Agency Space Debris Coordination Committee, has resulted in the adoption of voluntary space guidelines to be followed by space powers. These guidelines should help limit the proliferation of space debris, yet for the time being it is feared that the creation of such debris will continue to outpace mitigation efforts.[20]

b) Threat of Weapons

Despite the worrying consequences of the environmental threats currently taunting this unique community realm, there exist even more provocative threats that must be addressed with priority. These threats deal as discussed above, with the use of force in outer space. It may be helpful at this point, to make a clear distinction between the *militarization* and *weaponization* of space. The militarization of space means the use of space for military purposes; the use of satellites for communications, command and control, navigation (with global positioning system), reconnaissance and monitoring, as well as early warning systems.[21] The use of space for such military purposes has occurred since the first satellites were launched into orbit over fifty years ago.[22] On the other hand, the *weaponization* of space would mean the placement in orbit of satellites with independent destructive capacities.[23] The prospect of the deployment of such satellites possessing destructive capacities in space is one that causes much concern for many space experts as well as governments of our international community. The weaponization of space would undoubtedly have devastating consequences on outer space activities; consequences that would be felt in every corner of this world. The threat of space weaponization is confounded exponentially by the inevitable space arms race that would follow.[24] It is thus the threat of space weaponization and the possibility of an arms race that will be the focus of this report from here on in.

ANALYZING THE THREAT OF SPACE WEAPONIZATION

a) Defining 'space weapons'

Creating an accurate and comprehensive definition of what constitutes a space weapon, is, as was the case for defining outer space security, a challenging endeavor. In creating a space weapon definition, there are many ambiguous parameters that must be addressed. Such parameters include defining the boundaries of space; at how many meters above the Earth's surface, does space begin? Other questions bring up the issue of where the satellite must be situated and what kind of targets it must aim at, in order for it to be considered a space weapon. Must it hold solely destructive functions in order to be considered a weapon or are normally peaceful weapons with latent destructive capacities also considered a weapon? As is

---

[20] West "Back to the Future: The Outer Space Treaty turns 40".
[21] S. Estabrooks « Opposing weapons in space »
[22] Arbatov 105.
[23] S. Estabrooks « Opposing weapons in space »
[24] Jusheng 62.

self-evident, the question of space weapons is quite complex, and thus understandably, no clear consensus on the exact definition of a space weapon has been reached. However a generally accepted definition is that a space weapon is one that can attack land, sea, air or space targets while being situated in space; having orbited the Earth at least once, or having a stable station beyond earth orbit.[25] The Canadian government further specifies three categories of potential space weapons. These include space strike or orbital bombardment weapons, anti-satellite weapons (ASAT), and space-based variants of ballistic missile defense. The space strike or orbital bombardment weapons would be ones that attack land, sea or air targets from space, whereas ASAT weapons would attack other satellites orbiting in space. On the other hand, space-based variants of ballistic missile defense would have the capacity to from their location in space, destroy ballistic missiles during flight.[26] There exist also, however, other widely used definitions of space weapons such as that stated by Russian academic and politician, Alexei Arbatov as "attack munitions that have been created and tested for striking any target, and that operate from space objects, as well as attack munitions that have been created and tested for striking space object".[27] This latter definition would thus include Earth-based ASAT weapons as constituting a space weapon seeing as it attacks space objects.

b) Consequences of the existence and use of space weapons

The perils of the weaponization of space are often said to be only comparable with those of nuclear weapons, however, such claims cannot be confirmed since there has never been a direct military confrontation in this realm.[28] Yet even without taking into account the speculated devastating consequences of the use of space weapons, the mere existence of weapons in space is considered by many experts to be the most serious and immediate threat to outer space security. Due to the anarchic nature of the international system, the competition and mistrust inherent to such a system, would mean that the placing of any weapons in space would inevitably be followed by similar acts by different states, thus inducing an arms race.[29] The act of placing weapons in space can very easily be interpreted as an act of aggression and this would have disastrous effects on the trusting and cooperative international efforts made by the international space community. The destruction of such trust and cooperation between countries would in turn have devastating consequences for space activities which depend on inter-state cooperation, and so would of course also have an impact on the billions of people who have grown dependent on the modern-day benefits that space technology provides them with.[30] As for the consequences tied to the actual *use* of space weapons, the fact that immense damage would result, is evident. The use of weapons in space would not impact uniquely its target, but all spacecraft operating in that orbit. This is due to the fact that the debris created by the destruction of a satellite, will remain in that same

---

[25] S. Estabrooks « Opposing weapons in space »
[26] Ibid.
[27] Arbatov 87.
[28] Cesar Jaramillo,« In defence of the PPWT Treaty: Toward a space weapons ban," *The Ploughshares Monitor,* 30.4 (2009):Web
[29] Jusheng 62.
[30] Ibid.

orbit, thus increasing the chances of collisions. The seriousness of such consequences is well portrayed by the recent spacecraft destructions that have occurred (Chinese ASAT test and explosion of Russian rocket body, 2007). The amount of large space debris in popular orbits, increased by 20% from these two events alone. This figure demonstrates the large amount of space debris that deliberate satellite destruction causes, in relation to the 'natural' creation of space debris.[31] Having discussed the danger that space debris poses to orbiting satellites, the graveness of the consequences caused by possible future use of weapons in space, should be quite clear. The deployment of space weapons threatens not only this vast and important environment, but it threatens to endanger life as we know it.

c) Preventative measures taken against space weaponization

Outer Space Treaty

Officially named the "Treaty on the Principles Governing the Activities of States in the Exploration and use of Outer Space, Including the Moon and other Celestial Bodies", the Outer Space Treaty (OST) was signed on January 27th, 1967 in Moscow, London, and Washington.[32] With the USA and the USSR as its major authors, the treaty set the basic foundation for current international law, and is considered by many to be the corner stone of outer space governance.[33]

The OST aims to ensure the peaceful use of outer space for the benefit of all peoples and insists on the principle that outer space is not subject to any national claims of sovereignty. It also emphasizes the importance of international peace and security, and promotes international cooperation and understanding. Although the goal of the treaty is to ensure the peaceful use of space, the treaty only bans the outer space use of nuclear weapons or other weapons of mass destruction. There is no reference made to the use of conventional weapons in outer space and this proves to be a major flaw in this piece legal framework.[34] Aside from evident gaps in the treaty (such as the one mentioned above), there are several issues that arise due to the treaty's lack of 'definitional clarity'[35] for certain terms. One of the issues is that the treaty does not specify where airspace ends and outer space begins (The commonly accepted view now is that space begins at 100 km above the Earth). Another ambiguity that has proven to be equally problematic, is the wording of "peaceful purposes" used to describe activities permitted in space. The vagueness of this term has resulted in different interpretations of what exactly 'peaceful purposes' implies. Russia esteems that the wording means completely non-military uses of outer space, whereas the USA has chosen to interpret the term as meaning "non-aggressive" use of space.[36] Such ambiguities and the tensions they cause, create evident obstacles in the reinforcing of the OST's rules.

[31] West "Back to the Future: The Outer Space Treaty turns 40".
[32] Arbatov 50.
[33] West "Back to the Future: The Outer Space Treaty turns 40".
[34] Arbatov 50.
[35] Space Security 2010 60.
[36] Ibid.

The fact that to this date, no weapons have been placed in outer space is often emphasized by OST promoters to argue the importance of treaties in controlling weapons proliferation. Yet one must analyze this fact critically and question whether this absence of space weapons is truly due to this often considered outdated treaty, or maybe more related to technological limits that to this point have hindered the rapid deployment of weapons in this relatively unknown field. Given the great technological changes that have taken place over the past forty years, the OST fails now, more than ever before, to address the threats and challenges facing the conduct of outer space today.[37]

ABM Treaty

The "Treaty on the Limitation of Anti-Ballistic Missile Systems"(ABM Treaty)was a treaty signed between the USA and the USSR in 1972. The treaty was mainly concerned with limiting and reducing nuclear weapons, however also represented an important step towards controlling space militarization, as it prohibited development, testing and deployment of Ballistic Missile Defense (BMD) systems and space-based BMD components.[38]

The ABM Treaty could be viewed in some ways as an improvement of the OST concerning the issue of addressing the ban of weapons in space because the wording of the treaty does not restrict the limitations it imposes, to solely nuclear weapons. The limitations could therefore be applied to all other space-based weapons. Obeyed by both the USA and the Soviet Union administrations, the treaty proved to be effective in limiting BMD development and indirectly space weapons development until its dissolution by the Bush regime in 2002.[39] The abolishment of a previously relatively well-functioning treaty was disheartening to disarmament promoters worldwide as President Bush's action undermined the legitimacy of binding treaties and thus had obvious negative consequences on the ability of restriction of the development and deployment of space weapons through international laws.[40]

CD & PAROS

The lack of an international treaty that dealt specifically with the issue of space weaponization, led to the creation of the "Prevention of an Arms Race in Outer Space" (PAROS) resolution in the early 1980's. The United Nations Conference on Disarmament (CD) –a UN negotiation mechanism- was tasked with overseeing negotiations on a multilateral agreement to support PAROS. Since creation of PAROS resolution in the early 1980s, it has had near-unanimous support from UN country members however US has consistently been in opposition of such a treaty and along with Israel began abstaining from voting on the resolution in 1995. The uncooperativeness of this superpower ultimately led to a frustrating diplomatic gridlock which has stalled PAROS negotiations since 1995.[41] The first negative vote was cast by the United States in 2005 with the justification that there is no

---

[37]West "Back to the Future: The Outer Space Treaty turns 40".
[38] Arbatov 51.
[39] Arbatov 106.
[40] Haitao 116.
[41] Space Security 2010 64.

threat of an arms race and therefore the PAROS resolution serves no purpose.[42] During the 2007 CD Session, the superpower continued its uncooperative behavior, insisting that existing international agreements concerning conduct in space provide adequate protection. After three years of voting against the PAROS resolution, the US in 2009, converted to abstaining. While an abstention is better than a negative vote, there is no doubt that the USA continues to be the culprit in the failure of this otherwise much supported treaty.[43]

PPWT

Given the failure of past efforts at creating an official law-binding treaty concerning space weaponization, another attempt was made with the draft "Treaty on Prevention of the Placement of Weapons in Outer Space and of the Threat or Use of Force against Outer Space Objects" (PPWT), jointly introduced by Russia and China at the CD in 2008. Despite several shortcomings, the PPWT is widely regarded as "the most highly structured state-originating proposal that has been introduced in the CD with the aim of preventing the weaponization of space."[44] The goal of the treaty is to ban two interrelated conducts; that of the placement of weapons in outer space, and the threat or use of force against outer space objects. Some experts argue that the PPWT, unlike previous treaties, provides comprehensive and clear definitions of what constitutes a space weapon and also outlines in details what behavior is to be considered 'aggressive action'. However, others, such as Alexei Arbatov criticize the definition as being too ambiguous. Furthermore, the EU whilst appreciating the Sino-Russian efforts, state that the treaty is inadequate due to its lack of robust verification measures as well as its failure to address the issue of ASATs.[45] Nevertheless, this Russian-Chinese treaty initiative was well received by the international community, who saw the treaty as a practical solution to deal with the ongoing stalemate of the PAROS resolution. The biggest obstacle in the way of PPWT progress is the USA's staunch opposition to the treaty.[46] The PPWT, albeit relevant, comprehensive and approved by virtually all, risks the same fate as the PAROS resolution as it lies at the feet of the world's superpower.

Code of Conduct Approach

In light of the international community's consistent inability to create a ban on space weapons through binding treaties, experts are now turning toward a 'Code of Conduct' approach in order to solve the problem of treaties' often signature inhibiting 'detailed' rules of required behavior. A code of conduct, in contrast, constitutes of a list of non-binding space conduct guidelines that countries may choose to adopt and integrate in their national policies. Such an approach to space security has gained much recognition since the Council of the European Union published its proposed Code of Conduct for Outer Space at the end of 2008.[47] The EU Code of Conduct calls on states to use space for peaceful activities and to take measures to

---

[42] West « Fallout from China's anti-satellite test »
[43] Cesar Jaramillo, "In defence of the PPWT Treaty: Toward a space weapons ban".
[44] Ibid.
[45] Arbatov 91.
[46] Arbatov 84.
[47] Arbatov 75.

minimize the possibility of any damage being made to any space assets, whether that be accidentally or intentionally. The code also puts an emphasis on creating mechanisms to increase transparency and cooperation in outer space activities. The code does however fail to address some of the most controversial topics related to space security and there are those skeptical of its usefulness given that states are under no legal obligations to abide by the code's 'guidelines'. There are many, though, that view the code's non-binding nature as a way of harnessing greater international support which will ultimately lead to the progressive development of international law, and a possible stepping stone towards a more robust security regime.[48]

Whereas experts such as Wu Haitao insist that the best method for preventing an arms race in space is thru improving the current international legal systems on outer space and by creating a comprehensive international legal instrument specifically concerning the prevention of space weaponization (such as the PPWT created in 2008), I disagree with this conviction because of some inherent characteristics of treaties, which when placed in the anarchic context of the international system, make such prevention mechanisms futile.

The growing acceptance of using the code of conduct approach for creating space security is a strong indication of the perceived futileness of using a legal framework in order to control states' actions. Despite nearly fifty years of efforts made to control the security of outer space, contemporary international law does still not prohibit the placement of any non-nuclear weapons in space.[49] This fact reveals the existence of major flaws in the approaches that have been taken.

d) Effectiveness of preventative mechanisms

As has been made clear above by the overview of preventative measures taken towards space weaponization, the effectiveness of methods for preventing space weaponization and a possible space arms race has been unsettlingly poor. This I argue is due to general weaknesses tied to the international legal framework set up, as well as due to obstacles created by the uniqueness of the outer space situation.

The preventative mechanisms that have thus far been used have all been carried out in the international arena with the attempt of implementing an international legal framework to create a space security regime. In the specific case of treaties, there are in general three main challenges when attempting to create a legally binding treaty or resolution which states are expected to abide by. The first challenge with any treaty is to gather enough support to give it momentum. Such momentum is often lacking in large part due to treaties often being perceived as too restricting. Many states, especially the USA, are not willing to sign any binding international agreements that they feel puts too much restraint on their policies. A striking example of such state behavior can be observed for the international community's conduct concerning missiles. In 1987, a "Missile Technology Control Regime" treaty was

---

[48] Jaramillo, Cesar. « New Competition for a space security regime." *The Ploughshares Monitor.* 31.2 (2010):Web.
[49] Arbatov 82.

adopted. Only 34 nations joined; the others claiming that the treaty's restrictions were too strict as well as unverifiable. However, a code of Conduct against Ballistic Missile Proliferation adopted in 2002 has gathered the support of more than 120 states.[50] This example clearly displays the hesitance of many nations to engage in an agreement too strictly defined.

The second challenge stems from the fact that many treaties or resolutions and their content are dependent on unanimous consent by the parties involved. This makes it extremely difficult for anything to get accomplished as even the objection of one party, means that no real progress on the matter can be made. The uncompromising position of the United State concerning numerous international agreement efforts has provided proof for this point. Notably, due to the United States objection to the PAROS resolution, negotiation talks have remained stalled for over a decade, despite over 100 countries fully supporting the resolution's content. Thus the non-cooperation of less than one percent of the voting mass can result in no progress being made.[51]

The third challenge is that there is nothing really making 'binding treaties', binding. As the Bush regime's dissolution of the ABM Treaty in 2002 clearly showed, if a state no longer wants to abide to a legal agreement it has made, it simply doesn't.[52] The fact that treaties can be abolished at any point in time, takes away from its credibility as a legitimate tool for creating international laws.

Due to these three challenges/issues, the legal mechanisms put in place have not been very constructive in preventing the weaponization of space.

The already obstacle-filled treaty approach for preventing space weaponization is further hindered by the unique challenges that the characteristics off the outer space realm pose. The three most notable problems that this field provides are all tied to the relative recentness of the use of this last frontier as well as the complexity of technology involved in this use. The first issue concerns the ambiguity surrounding the exact definition of space weapon. Whereas any successful disarmament negotiations to date established a set of mutually agreed upon, clearly defined and specifically identified technical characteristics that characterize the weapons in question, space weapons are currently defined by the environment in which the weapon or target is situated rather than by specific technical traits.[53] Any legitimate treaty would need to take into account the "full potential for the development of space weapons, the scope of use, and their placement in orbit,"[54] and explicitly state these details in the treaty. The issues that

[50] Arbatov 71.
[51] S. Estabrooks « Opposing weapons in space »
[52] Arbatov 106.
[53] Arbatov 89.
[54] Sarah Estabrooks, "Update on a prevention of an Arms Race in Outer Space," *The Ploughshares Monitor*, 27.3 (2006):Web.

the current ambiguity of the space weapon definition create, are similar to those emerging due to the vagueness of the term 'peaceful purposes' as was discussed above.

The second obstacle concerns the issue of verification. Being able to verify the rules set out in a legal framework is imperative if it is to have any sort of legitimacy. The problem concerning international laws on outer space is that they are extremely difficult to verify. Carrying out verification measures can be complicated in any situation, however the vast and unique outer space environment confront such measures with unprecedented obstacles. The unique challenges of identifying supposed banned spacecraft among the more than 700 currently orbiting Earth as well as the profound complexity of being able to verify that the identified object does indeed possess characteristics that fall under the 'banned objects' list, makes verification of treaty obeyance near impossible. Given the imperativeness of credible verification procedures in order to make any treaty binding, the unique outer space situation makes any form of treaty basically useless.[55]

A third challenge that has undermined the to-date space weaponization preventative measures that have been taken is the issue of transparency. Countries such as China have been extremely secretive about their space programs.[56] Such secretive behavior hurts the chances of international cooperation as it may cause other states to question the secretive countries activities, creating distrust. The fundamental base for any cooperation is that of trust; and secrets do not provide a welcoming environment for such trust. Thus the lack of space activity transparency caused by some countries further weakens the already emasculated preventative mechanisms used to this date.

It has been widely agreed upon, that having a well-defined and clearly laid out subject of agreement, accompanied by realistic and reliable transparency and verification measures, is crucial to the success of any negotiations for an international agreement.[57] Taking into consideration the challenges the question of space creates, it should be clear that it is not through an international legal framework that space weaponization will be prevented.

The recent international trend towards establishing a code of conduct on outer space use has been received with enthusiasm by some. At first glance, it seems to provide a solution to the main issues that characterize international treaties and resolutions. By being voluntary and consisting of general conduct guidelines, a code of conduct by-steps the roadblocks set by being too restrictive or requiring signatures in order to be recognized. Seen as a possible stepping stone towards a more rigid space security regime, the code of conduct method is a positive development. Nevertheless, we must not forget that what drives states acts is not the desire to cooperate with others, but their need to satisfy their national interests. [58]Thus, although a code of conduct may gain the support of the world community and have the

---

[55] Arbatov 94.
[56] Ashley Tellis, "China's Space Capabilities and U.S. Security Interests," *Carnegie Endowment*. Oct. 2008, Web.
[57] Arbatov 98.
[58] Tim Dunne, *International Relations Theory,* Hampshire: Oxford University Press, 2010.

capacity to create international norms, it takes only one uncooperative country to break the fragile bond of cooperation and trust that this code of conduct method strives to create.

Thus I argue that the use of the international legal framework or an attempt at the creation of international cooperation, as a preventative method in the struggle to keep outer space weapons free, is ultimately of little use. One can create as many treaties or codes of conduct as one wishes, but in the end it will always come down to a state's national interest as it is a state's national interest that is the driving force behind a state's actions. The reason that national interest drives some states to pursue aggressive policies while others opt for cooperation is based on the balance of power. Countries with hegemonic aspirations will consistently have unilateral policies whereas weaker states' national interests will be more focused on cooperating with other weaker nations in order to ensure their national interest (in this case security), against more powerful aggressive states. Any preventative mechanism used must thus incorporate a way in which to make the integrity of a state's national interest a conditional part of the equation.

Historically, national interest has been dominated by the need for military force. However, given the capitalist structure in which we live today, economic strength has come to play an increasingly important role. The logic behind this is quite simple: in order to ensure a nation's well-being, a state needs capital resources in order to make its society function. The health of the economy is therefore essential in satisfying a state's national interest.[59] Given this fact, a more effective way of ensuring space security would be to effect economic sanctions on any countries not following the rules decided on by a *majority* (not unanimous). Such a system would keep the few power greedy countries objecting to the rules ensuring global space security, in check seeing as they risked undermining their own national interest by stepping out of line.

This, results however, in a catch-22 situation in which in order for the economic sanctions to be effective, cooperation would be needed from the powers on which the sanctions would be imposed. This stems quite simply from the fact that the states vying for aggressive security are most often the ones possessing the most power as well as wealth. Imposing such sanctions on powers could risk at times being more damaging to the ensemble of weaker states than to the powers who, given their superior position, would be able to use leverage to punish those going against them. The only way that economic sanctions may be viable would be if an aggressive power was faced with the complete international community cohesively implementing the sanctions; if any were to not cooperate all legitimacy would be lost. Given the diversity of the international political landscape, it would seem near impossible to succeed in having all states take action against one. My conclusion, albeit pessimistic, is thus that no system will truly prevent states from doing what they want; even if their actions were to endanger the planet. States' indifference to the peril it can threaten humanity with was made clear during the Cold War in which both the US and the USSR unwaveringly placed national interest before global security.

---

[59] Ibid.

At this time it may be relevant thus to discuss the recent international situation concerning outer space, as the international environment evidently has a large impact in the actions taken for a state's national interest. Following an overview of the current trends relating to outer space, it will be of importance to assess the national space policies and the attitudes of three states which have a considerable influence on the world scene; the US, China and Russia.

e) Current Trends in the International Community

In the past few decades, states such as Canada, China, France, Germany, India, Israel, Italy, Spain and the UK have joined Russia and US in developing military space capabilities (especially in the area of surveillance). However, no overt interest in the development of space weapons has been made clear by these states. The international community, with the notable exception of the United States, has been very supportive and cooperative in working towards a space weapons ban. Even countries such as Russia and China, widely viewed as military powers and rivals of the US have opted to take public action in efforts to ban space weapons. The European Union has a strong space program focused on scientific discovery and after the US, has the greatest commercial and scientific interest in space.[60] It also is a strong advocate for international cooperation concerning the use of space for peaceful purposes, as was made clear by the union's drafting of the EU Code of Conduct for Outer Space Activities.[61] Given the international community support existing for cooperation in outer space, it may seem surprising that military as well as political tensions concerning outer space are rising.[62] However, this phenomenon is not without reason. Given certain actions taken by certain countries over the past decade and taking into consideration the increasing dependence that nations around the world have on space, it is natural that securitizing one's assets in space is becoming an increasing concern. The attempted rocket launches by North Korea in 2006 and 2009, the Chinese ASAT test in 2007, the US targeting of one of its dysfunctional satellites in 2008, as well as the accidental collision of a US and a Russian spacecraft in 2009, all create justifiable concern regarding certain state's true intentions as well as concerns about the additional space debris undermining contemporary security.[63]

Despite worldwide consent for the need for cooperation, there remains a reserve of distrust towards other countries' motives as is reflected in the European Union's Space Strategy which states that in order to ensure the security of EU citizens, it will "[take] full advantage of dual-use synergies as appropriate."[64] This distrust stems naturally from the inherent anarchic nature of the international system in which states can never fully trust each other, and is exacerbated by the national military policies of certain states, notably those of the U.S., Russia and China.

---

[60]S. Estabrooks « Opposing weapons in space »
[61] Space Security 2010 75.
[62]West "Back to the Future: The Outer Space Treaty turns 40".
[63] West, "Anarchy in space: The need for a comprehensive security regime for outer space." *The Ploughshares Monitor.* 30.2 (2009):Web.
[64]EU Space Strategy
http://ec.europa.eu/enterprise/policies/space/files/policy/comm_native_com_2011_0152_6_communication_en.pdf

Ranging from outright aggressive, to conditionally cooperative, the space policies of these three world military powers will play a large role in the future developments concerning space weaponization.

USA

The imperialist nature of the United States national and foreign policies means that it has traditionally not been willing to cooperate with other nations on matters such as state security, as it seems to consider itself above the law concerning most matters in general. Such an attitude means that this superpower has always been a major obstacle to any attempts towards securitizing space. It has been an obstacle not only in the sense that it has prevented any international legal progress concerning space weaponization to advance, but also in the sense that its aggressive policies brew insecurity which can lead to similar actions being taken up by other states.

The US has by far the most developed space capabilities and is the most dependent on the use of outer space technology. This should not be surprising seeing as this country accounts for 90% of world-wide space military spending.[65]

The 1997 US SPACECOM document Vision for 2020 created by the Clinton regime, clearly stated its desire to be dominant in all spheres and thus outlined a new military vision to dominate space.[66] This vision was carried forward by the Bush administration who was very clear about its goals to weaponize space, making statements such as US John Mohanco's at an informal debate on PAROS 2006: "As long as the potential for such attacks [on satellites] remains, our Government will continue to consider the possible role that space-related weapons may play in protecting our assets."[67]

The Clinton and Bush regimes' aggressive approach to outer space use created much tension and a sense of insecurity which countries like China and Russia have vowed to counter by taking aggressive approaches as well. Cautious hope has however been born with Obama's regime who's Space Security policy appears to be less aggressive, hinting towards support for the banning of certain types of space weapons, while also advocating the need for international cooperation concerning outer space issues.[68] Critiques have however pointed out that Obama's space policies are vague and do not outright commit to any sort of positive actions, while also raising the point that Obama's statements may be a simple attempt to calm the international communities concerns concerning US space policy. Given its history, it will be hard for any state to trust in the goodwill of this hegemonic power when it comes down to choosing between international cooperation and national interest.

---

[65]Cesar Jaramillo, "Space Security Fact Sheet"
[66]S. Estabrooks « Opposing weapons in space »
[67] Estabrooks "Update on a prevention of an Arms Race in Outer Space." *The Ploughshares Monitor*. 27.3 (2006):Web.
[68]Space Security 2010 68.

Russia

As one of the world's leading space powers, Russia has much interest in the continuous secure use of outer space, which explains Russian Ambassador to the CD, Valery Loschinin's statement in 2009 claiming that Russia's top priority was a prevention of an arms race in outer space.[69] The country seems to be especially concerned by the potential US deployment of a space component for the antimissile defense systems as this could substantially reduce the credibility of Russia's nuclear deterrence.[70] Given the threat that Russia feels from US policies concerning space, it is understandable that Russia has played such a prominent role in promoting international cooperation concerning space security. This attempt at international cooperation must however be interpreted realistically; Russia is willing to cooperate if such behavior could prevent states such as the US from placing weapons in space. However, were weapons to be placed in space, Russia has been quite insistent on making it clear that it too would then follow down this path of no return.[71]

China

China's stance concerning outer space as its public discourse is not completely consistent with some of its actions taken. Furthermore, its space program is masked by a thick veil of secrecy, being described by some as a "mystery within a maze,"[72]which makes it extremely difficult to decipher the country's true intentions. On the one hand, China has taken on the role, alongside Russia, as one of the most active promoters of the banning of space weapons, as is shown notably with its co-creation of the PPWT. However one cannot ignore China's ASAT test in early 2007, which has been surrounded by much speculation.[73] Given China's known ambitions for becoming a world power, one must be conscientious of the fact that it is not realistic to assume that the PRC would let other states gain a military advantage over them if at all possible. Indeed, China has threatened that if the USA were to proceed with space weaponization, it would respond in the same manner.[74] The hypocritical behavior of the Chinese government has prompted much confusion as well as suspicion regarding the country's true space motives. In a world in which we err on caution, it is not surprising that the PRC's inconsistencies have provoked political fall outs and have left other states wary of its actions.

f) Theoretical Application

Current trends have shown overall commitment to international cooperation; however the contradictory and at times vaguely defined space ambitions of three of the world's powers leave room for concern regarding space security.

---

[69] Ibid 69.
[70] Arbatov 43.
[71]Space Security 2010 81.
[72] Ashley Tellis, "China's Space Capabilities and U.S. Security Interests".
[73] Arbatov 6.
[74] S. Estabrooks « Opposing weapons in space »

As was made clear above, the prevention measures haven't worked and will not work with the underlying reason for all of the failed measures being that a state will always act out of national interest and not for others. It was thus established that the weaponization of space is inevitable. I will now use a structural realist concept called the 'security dilemma' in order to explain why the inevitable weaponization in space will result in the inevitability of an outer space arms race. The basic principles of the security dilemma are based on the structure of the international state system. The creator of this concept, John Herz, argues that given the anarchic environment in which states exist, each state can only count on itself for its own survival. This means that a state (A) constantly needs to assure that it is not militarily inferior to another state, as this could spell death for it. Therefore, state A will always be working to strengthen its military in order to increase its security. However by increasing its security, state A undermines the security of the other states who, never fully being able to trust other countries, will interpret the strengthening of state A's military as an aggressive act. This in turn means that the other states, in order to ensure their own security, will begin to strengthen their military capabilities as well. This creates a vicious circle of military strengthening whose main culprits are mistrust and the consequential perception of insecurity.[75]

Characteristics of such a security dilemma are observable in the current international environment today. Despite efforts for cooperation, there remains a haze of distrust surrounding the issue of space security, which causes each state to fear for its security. Such fears as many experts have stated will lead to states with the capacity to secretly develop space weapons as a defensive measure against potential threats.[76] Evidence of such developments is readily available if we take for example the Chinese ASAT test in 2007. This event had a negative impact on the country's political relations notably with that of the United States, who in 2008 executed its own ASAT test.[77] The Chinese ASAT test, surrounded by secrecy, could be viewed as a sign of Chinese interest in space weapons, which could be interpreted as having been influenced by the Bush regime's overt aggressive space policy. The insecurity of China, which most likely caused the testing, in turn caused insecurity for the US.[78] Thus here we can see the beginnings of a security dilemma, which will most likely pull several countries into its downward spiral. Due to the constant perceived insecurity, weapons in space would thus be in constant need of improvement. The phenomenon that this space security dilemma would provoke, could be likened to that of the Cold War in which having nuclear weapons was not enough; there was always the fear that the enemy would create a more advanced version.[79]

The mature outcome of such a security dilemma would inevitably be an arms race in outer space. This prediction gains even more credibility when we take into consideration public

---

[75] Battistella 511-516.
[76] S. Estabrooks « Opposing weapons in space »
[77] Ashley Tellis, "China's Space Capabilities and U.S. Security Interests".
[78] West "Fallout from China's anti-satellite test"
[79] Schell

statements by both China and Russia who have hinted at their ambitions for space weaponization, were a country such as the US to deploy a weapon in outer space.[80]

In conclusion, the turn of this millennium could be viewed as the calm before the storm. Mankind currently enjoys significant benefits from its use of outer space. Yet despite the urgent call made by many countries for a prevention of the weaponization of space, it is clear that it is only a matter of time before the world will bear witness to exactly that. This report has documented the repeated failure of preventative measures to make any real progress towards the prevention of the deployment of space weapons. Albeit, no such weapons existing so far, John Herz's security dilemma provides a convincing prediction of how this space security struggle will play out. This gloomy prediction may be viewed by some as pessimistic, however one should rather heed and take this report for what it is: a realistic prediction of our Earth's future based on historical facts and centuries of theorists' observation of state's behavior in this chaotic world we all call home.

---

[80]S. Estabrooks « Opposing weapons in space »

BIBLIOGRAPHY

Arbatov, Alexei. *Outer Space : Weapons, Diplomacy and Security.* Washington D.C.: Union Book Press, 2010.

Battistella, Dario. *Théories des relations internationales.* Paris: Sciences Po Les Presses, 2009.

Brinton, Turner. "Obama's Proposed Space Weapon Ban Draws Mixed responses." *Space News.* 04 Feb. 2009, Web.

Dunne, Tim. *International Relations Theory.* Hampshire: Oxford University Press, 2010.

Estabrooks, Sarah. "Opposing Weapons in space." *The Ploughshares Monitor.* 23.3 (2002):Web.

Estabrooks, Sarah. "Preventing the weaponization of space : options for moving forward." Project Ploughshares, Mar. 2003, Web.

Estabrooks, Sarah. "Update on a prevention of an Arms Race in Outer Space." *The Ploughshares Monitor.* 27.3 (2006):Web.

Haitao, Wu. "An effective way to preserve the security and prevent an arms race in outer space to negotiate and conclude an international legal instrument at an early date." *Building the Architecture for Sustainable Space Security.* UNIDIR, 2006.

Jaramillo, Cesar. « In defence of the PPWT Treaty: Toward a spzce weapons ban." *The Ploughshares Monitor.* 30.4 (2009):Web.

Jaramillo, Cesar. « New Competition for a space security regime." *The Ploughshares Monitor.* 31.2 (2010):Web.

Jaramillo, Cesar. "Space Security Fact Sheet" *Space Security Index,* 2010, Web.

Jusheng, Pan. "Addressing the Outer Space Security Issue." *Building the Architecture for Sustainable Space Security.* UNIDIR, 2006.

Schell, Jonathan. *The Seventh Decade: The New Shape of Nuclear Danger.* New York: Metropolitan Books, 2007.

Space Security Index. *Space Security 2010.* Waterloo, 2010.

Tellis, Ashley. "China's Space Capabilities an U.S.Security Interests." *Carnegie Endowment.* Oct. 2008, Web.

West, Jessica. "Back to the future: The Outer Space Treaty turns 40." *The Ploughshares Monitor.* 28.3 (2007):Web.

West, Jessica. "Reaching out: New approaches to security in space." *The Ploughshares Monitor.* 30.1 (2009):Web.

West, Jessica. "Fallout from China's anti-satellite test." *The Ploughshares Monitor.* 28.1 (2007):Web.

West, Jessica. "Anarchy in space: The need for a comprehensive security regime for outer space." *The Ploughshares Monitor.* 30.2 (2009):Web.